classical composers

compiled and edited by **Michael Aston**

MUSIC DEPARTMENT

OXFORD
UNIVERSITY PRESS

OXFORD
UNIVERSITY PRESS

Great Clarendon Street, Oxford OX2 6DP, England
198 Madison Avenue, New York, NY 10016, USA

Oxford University Press is a department of the University of Oxford.
It furthers the University's aim of excellence in research, scholarship,
and education by publishing worldwide in

Oxford New York

Auckland Cape Town Hong Kong Karachi
Kuala Lumpur Madrid Melbourne Mexico City Nairobi
New Delhi Shanghai Taipei Toronto

With offices in

Argentina Austria Brazil Chile Czech Republic France Greece
Guatemala Hungary Italy Japan Poland Portugal Singapore
South Korea Switzerland Thailand Turkey Ukraine Vietnam

Oxford is a registered trade mark of Oxford University Press
in the UK and in certain other countries

1 3 5 7 9 10 8 6 4 2

ISBN 978-0-19-335919-2

Music origination by
Enigma Music Production Services, Amersham, Bucks.
Printed in Great Britain on acid-free paper by
Halstan & Co. Ltd., Amersham, Bucks.

contents

Introduction and Notes on the Pieces   4

J. C. F. Bach: Allegro con spirito from Sonata in A major   6

L. van Beethoven: Sonata in D major, Op. 6
Allegro molto   20
Rondo: moderato   30

Muzio Clementi: Allegro maestoso from Sonata in
E♭ major, Op. 3 No. 2   40

Joseph Haydn: Minuet and Trio from Symphony
No. 100 'Military'   52

W. A. Mozart: Allegro from Serenade K388   58

Franz Schubert: Entr'acte No. 3 from *Rosamunde*   66

introduction

The Classical period saw a substantial growth of interest in the medium of the piano duet as the pianoforte increasingly superseded the harpsichord as the favoured keyboard instrument. There is a wealth of original duet music dating from the era, starting with compositions by the sons of J. S. Bach and moving through to the great masterpieces of Mozart and Schubert. For this album a selection has been made that covers a period of around forty years and includes both original duets and arrangements. Original duets by Haydn, Mozart, and Schubert are already readily available for performers, and for this reason new arrangements of larger works have been included in their place, allowing for greater variety within the volume. These sit happily alongside original duet sonata movements by J. C. F. Bach and Clementi, and Beethoven's complete Sonata in D major, which serves as an ideal concert work.

Michael Aston, Leeds, 2007

notes on the pieces

J. C. F. Bach: Allegro con spirito from Sonata in A major

Johann Christoph Friedrich Bach (1732–95) was the sixteenth child of Johann Sebastian Bach. He worked at the court in Bückeburg for most of his life, and produced a sizeable output of compositions in many genres. The Sonata in A major for four hands was composed in 1786. In 1778 J. C. F. Bach travelled to England, and he returned to Germany with an English piano. It is therefore quite possible that the duet sonata was written with piano rather than harpsichord in mind.

A metronome mark of $\downarrow = c.64$ would allow the 'con spirito' feel of the music to be achieved, and a light touch with crisp finger-work is needed to give the required sparkle to the movement. There is a danger of the semiquaver passages sounding heavy when they occur in the lower registers of the keyboard, so the secondo player needs to take particular care to preserve clarity. The movement's natural momentum is best achieved if the pulse is consistently maintained.

L. van Beethoven: Sonata in D major, Op. 6

Ludwig van Beethoven (1770–1827) composed only a small amount of music for piano duet, and the Sonata in D major dates from 1796–7. This was a time when Beethoven's skills as a pianist were gaining recognition, and when he was composing primarily for the piano.

For the lively first movement, a speed of $\downarrow. = c.66$ would work well. The minuet style of the movement would have appealed to Viennese players, and this dancing quality must be maintained throughout. The two parts are treated with equality, and there are some charming passages of dialogue that should be enjoyed to the full. Beethoven's performance markings are plentiful and should be followed closely. The unusual use of hairpins in bars 26–8 (and elsewhere) raises questions for performers; one solution would be to crescendo up to the third beat in each bar to provide a match in dynamics for the *sf* markings in bars 30–2.

The 'dolce' mood of the second movement suggests a tempo in the region of $\downarrow = 116$. There should be no sense of hurrying, even in the faster passages. The accompaniment shared by primo left hand and secondo right hand in, for example, bars 1–8 needs to provide a gently rippling background to the lilting melody—passages such as this would benefit from separate practising, as perfection of ensemble is called for! When the texture thickens at bar 66 it is vital to avoid any heaviness that might destroy the quality of the melodic line.

Muzio Clementi: Allegro maestoso from Sonata in E♭ major, Op. 3 No. 2

Muzio Clementi (1752–1832) composed a large amount of keyboard music, including several sonatas for piano duet. The Sonata in E♭ major was written in 1779 and is among the earliest examples of original duet music from the Classical period.

The presence of the word 'maestoso' suggests that Clementi had in mind a tempo that would allow the often lyrical nature of the movement to shine through. A metronome mark of ♩ = 114 would suit this aspect of the piece, and would cater well for the faster passages. Clementi provided markings for basic changes in dynamic level, but there is scope within these for further subtle shading. He was less precise with phrasing indications, so editorial suggestions have been added. The semiquaver passages need clean articulation and brightness of tone to provide a good contrast with the flowing legato of the melodic lines.

Joseph Haydn: Minuet and Trio

Joseph Haydn (1732–1809) enjoyed great success in England in the late 1700s, and it was during a tour to the country in 1794 that his 100th symphony was heard for the first time. Known as the 'Military', the symphony quickly became one of his most popular works.

The Minuet and Trio movement has all the gracefulness and lilt that characterize Haydn's dance music, and these should be highlighted when performing the duet arrangement. The tempo should be steady—perhaps ♩ = c.120. In the minuet section, second beats should be kept light and slightly short, and the figure that opens the trio section will require strict rhythmic precision. Markings of phrasing and dynamics follow those given by Haydn in the original version.

W. A. Mozart: Allegro

Wolfgang Amadeus Mozart (1756–91) composed his Serenade K388 in 1782 or 1783. The work was originally scored for 2 oboes, 2 clarinets, 2 bassoons, and 2 horns, and in 1788 Mozart made an arrangement for string quintet; it is the original scoring that has been used as the source for this duet. Most of the Allegro (fourth movement) is ideally suited to arrangement for piano duet, but some sections proved less satisfying for this medium and have therefore been omitted.

A metronome mark of ♩ = c.110 should serve to accommodate the varying moods of this piece, which is effectively a set of variations on a theme. Some parts of the arrangement are a close transcription of the original, but other sections have been treated more freely. The duet should be approached pianistically, and suggestions have been made with regard to phrasing and articulation. The dynamic markings follow the broad indications given by Mozart in the original version. Above all, the contrast between the sections needs to be brought out in performance.

Franz Schubert: Entr'acte No. 3

Franz Schubert (1797–1828) composed his incidental music for Helmina von Chézy's play *Rosamunde, Fürstin von Zypern* in a very short space of time in December 1823. Some of the numbers in the collection became, and have remained, popular concert items in their own right.

A tempo of ♩ = c.75 would serve well for the underlying pulse of this piece. The 'maggiore' section needs to project a feeling of unhurried calm, and phrases must be allowed to breathe naturally. There is scope in this section for some judicious *rubato*. The first 'minore' section starts with a sense of greater urgency, and the tempo could move on a little more; Minore II has a richer texture, which should be enjoyed without losing the essentially light quality of the music. Suggestions for pedalling have not been made, and players should experiment with their own ideas. The 'maggiore' section in particular would benefit from the regular use of the pedal.

Allegro con spirito
from Sonata in A major

J. C. F. BACH
(1732–95)

Allegro con spirito
from Sonata in A major

J. C. F. BACH
(1732–95)

SECONDO

PRIMO

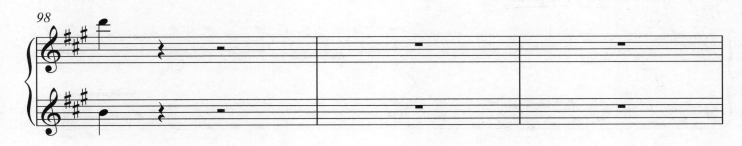

SECONDO

Sonata in D major, Op. 6

L. van BEETHOVEN
(1770–1827)

Sonata in D major, Op. 6

L. van BEETHOVEN
(1770–1827)

RONDO
Moderato

Secondo

RONDO
Moderato

Primo

Allegro maestoso
from Sonata in E♭ major, Op. 3 No. 2

MUZIO CLEMENTI
(1752–1832)

Allegro maestoso

Secondo

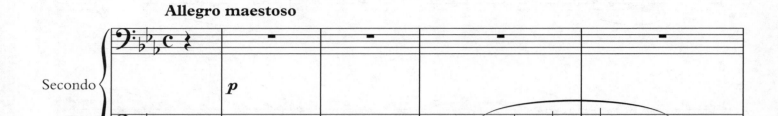

Allegro maestoso

from Sonata in E♭ major, Op. 3 No. 2

MUZIO CLEMENTI
(1752–1832)

41

Minuet and Trio
from Symphony No. 100 'Military'

JOSEPH HAYDN (1732–1809)
arranged by Michael Aston

MINUET
Moderato

Secondo

Minuet and Trio
from Symphony No. 100 'Military'

JOSEPH HAYDN (1732–1809)
arranged by Michael Aston

Allegro
from Serenade K388

W. A. MOZART (1756–91)
arranged by Michael Aston

Allegro
from Serenade K388

W. A. MOZART (1756–91)
arranged by Michael Aston

Primo

Entr'acte No. 3
from *Rosamunde*

FRANZ SCHUBERT (1797–1828)
arranged by Michael Aston

Entr'acte No. 3
from *Rosamunde*

FRANZ SCHUBERT (1797–1828)
arranged by Michael Aston

MINORE I

Maggiore D.C.
al Minore II